Solving Problems:
Dams, Bridges and Canals

Written by Kerrie Shanahan
Series Consultant: Linda Hoyt

WorldWise™
Content-based Learning

Contents

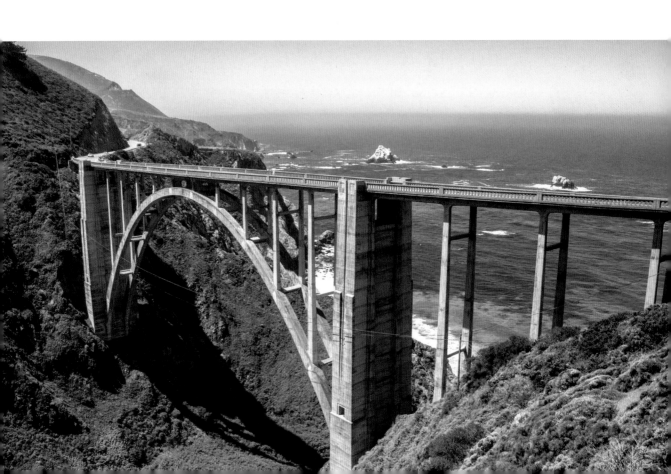

Seven Mile Bridge, Florida Keys, USA

Canal of Corinth, Greece

Roman bridge, Burgos, Spain

Introduction

Jindabyne Dam, New South Wales, Australia

Dams, bridges and canals were first built thousands of years ago. They were very simple **structures** built using the materials people found around them, such as wood, rock, stone and bamboo.

When concrete and steel became available, dams, bridges and canals became bigger, wider and stronger. As the need for larger and better structures arose, designs became more complex.

They have brought many benefits to people and communities. But, sometimes they have also had a negative impact on people and the environment.

Aldeadávila Dam in the River Duero, Spain

Panama Canal

Chapter 1

Building dams

Dams are built to store water. A simple dam can be dug out of the land to trap rainwater. Often, farmers build these to provide water for animals or crops.

Some dams are built as a barrier that stops the flow of water in a river. The stored water is then ready to be used when needed. These dams are often very large and form lakes or reservoirs.

Other dams are built to provide water to power stations to make electricity. This type of electricity is called **hydroelectricity**.

The water from dams can be piped downhill to nearby cities and towns.

Large dams need to be designed and built with strong materials like concrete so that the large volume of water does not leak and cause floods.

Famous dams

◀ The Hoover Dam is on the Colorado River in the United States. It was built in the 1930s and at that time was the tallest dam in the world. The stored water in the Hoover Dam is used to make electricity. It supplies power to 1.6 million homes.

▼ The Three Gorges Dam in China is the world's biggest dam. It is over one kilometre long and 60 storeys high. It took 40,000 workers 17 years to build. The dam was built to generate electricity. It also helps prevent flooding of the Yangtze River and makes it easier for ships to travel on the river.

Find out more

Where does the water in your home come from? Is it stored in a dam? Find out about a dam near your home.

Types of dams

There are different types of dams. Some of the main types are arch, buttress, embankment and gravity dams.

Arch dams

Arch dams are built where a river runs through a steep, narrow valley. Their curved shape is usually made of concrete. The rounded side of the dam holds back the water.

Buttress dams

Buttress dams have concrete walls that are supported by strong, triangular-shaped **structures**. These structures hold the water back.

Gordon Dam

The Gordon Dam on the Gordon River in Tasmania is used for hydroelectricity. It was opened in 1978 and is 140 metres high.

Oberon Dam

The Oberon Dam on the Fish River in New South Wales was built between 1954 and 1957 as part of the Fish River water supply scheme. It is made of reinforced concrete.

Embankment dams

Embankment dams have broad sloping sides that are made of rocks and soil. The weight of the rocks and soil holds back the water.

Gravity dams

Gravity dams have a straight side that faces the water. They are made of concrete. They must be strong enough to hold back the water with their own weight.

Corin Dam

Corin Dam is located in the Australian Capital Territory, on the Cotter River. It was built in 1968 to provide drinking water to Canberra.

Warragamba Dam

The Warragamba Dam is the main water supply for the city of Sydney. It took 12 years to build and was opened in 1960. The storage lake is four times bigger than Sydney Harbour.

Chapter 2

Building bridges

A bridge is a **structure** built to **span** a canyon, a river, a road or a lake. Bridges allow people, cars, trains and other vehicles to travel across these places.

Engineers who design bridges have many problems to solve. The bridge must be strong enough to hold the traffic that crosses it. It must also be long enough to span the river, road or other obstacle that it needs to cross.

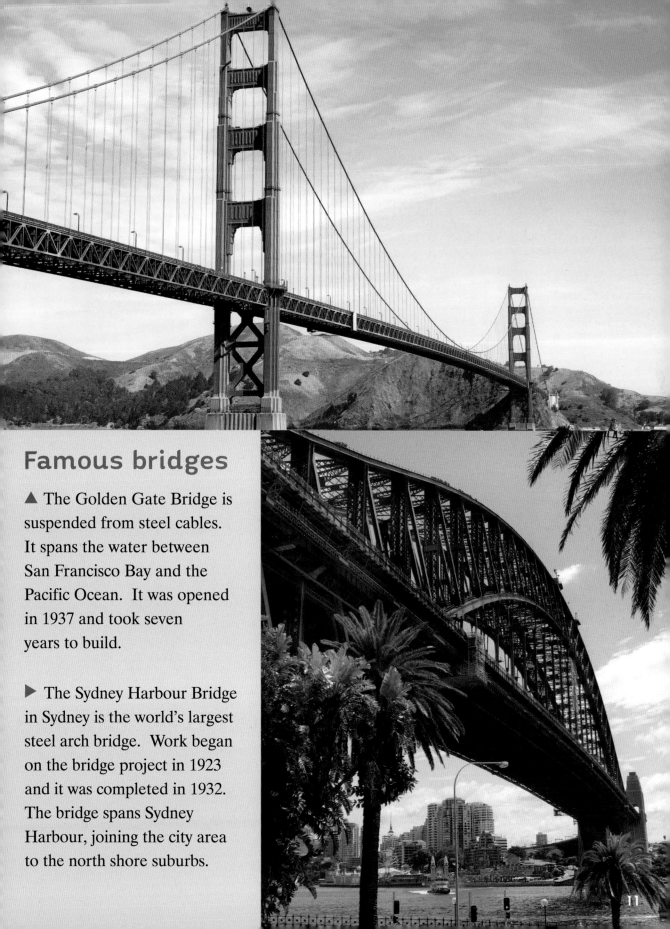

Famous bridges

▲ The Golden Gate Bridge is suspended from steel cables. It spans the water between San Francisco Bay and the Pacific Ocean. It was opened in 1937 and took seven years to build.

▶ The Sydney Harbour Bridge in Sydney is the world's largest steel arch bridge. Work began on the bridge project in 1923 and it was completed in 1932. The bridge spans Sydney Harbour, joining the city area to the north shore suburbs.

Types of bridges

There are different types of bridges. Some of the main types are beam, arch, truss and suspension bridges.

Beam bridges

A beam bridge is the simplest type of bridge. It has a horizontal beam supported at each end by piers. The first beam bridges were made of logs. Now concrete and steel are used.

Lake Ponchartrain Causeway

The Lake Ponchartrain Causeway in southern Louisiana in the United States is one of the longest beam bridges in the world. It is about 38 kilometres long.

Arch bridges

Arch bridges are made of one large or several small arches. Thousands of years ago they were made of stone, but today they are made of steel or concrete. The arch's curve makes It strong.

Ponte Vecchio

The Ponte Vecchio crosses the Arno River in Florence, Italy. It is a pedestrian bridge built over one thousand years ago.

Truss bridges

Truss bridges are a simple beam bridge that is made stronger by triangle shapes placed either above or below the beam. The triangle shapes were first made from wood but are now usually made from steel.

Astoria–Megler Bridge

The Astoria–Megler Bridge spans the Columbia River in Oregon. It is the longest continuous truss bridge in North America.

Suspension bridges

Suspension bridges are made up of a long beam with two or more tall towers. Cables are attached to the towers and run down to the beam. The cables help to support the bridge. Suspension bridges are light and strong.

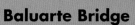

Baluarte Bridge

The Baluarte Bridge in Mexico is 402 metres high. It is a type of suspension bridge known as a cable-stayed bridge.

Chapter 3

Building canals

People have been building canals for over 5,000 years.
Canals are built for a variety of purposes.

To redirect water

Some canals are built to **redirect** fresh
water in rivers, lakes or streams. These
canals provide drinking water for people
or are used to **irrigate** crops.

To protect people

In the past, canals were sometimes
built to protect people living in a city.
The canal provided a barrier against
people wanting to attack and conquer
the city.

To connect bodies of water

Some canals are built for ships and boats
to travel on. Many of these canals connect
two bodies of water. They create a shortcut
for ships and make it easier for people and
goods to get from one place to another.

To transport food and goods

People build canals to connect parts of a town or two or more cities so that food and other goods can be more easily transported. Some canals allow boats and ships to travel inland where there was once no water to travel on.

How do canals work?

Engineers design canals. The engineer thinks about what the canal will be used for, how long and wide it needs to be, where it must go and how much it will cost.

Canals are built by digging a large **channel** that is filled with water. The canal is usually lined with materials such as stone, concrete or steel. These make the canal strong and stop the water from leaking out.

Famous canals

Many canals have changed how people live.

Grand Canal

The Grand Canal in China was one of the earliest major canals. Its first section was built about 2,600 years ago. It is the world's longest canal at 1,770 kilometres long and connects the Yangtze and Yellow Rivers.

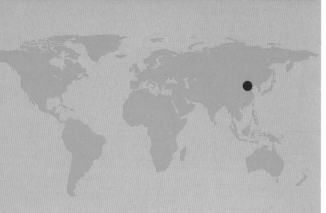

Choa Phraya River canals

In Bangkok, Thailand, the Choa Phraya River flows in a loop through canals. Many people live in houses on these canals and trade from boats called floating markets.

Erie Canal

The Erie Canal opened in New York in the United States in 1825. It connects the Hudson River and Lake Erie. It made the transporting of goods quicker, easier and cheaper. The canal also opened up the country to new areas where people could settle.

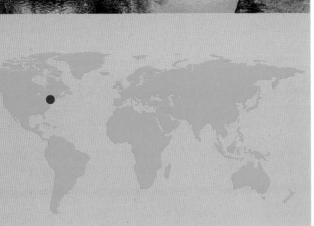

Suez Canal

The Suez Canal is one of the world's most famous canals. It was opened in Egypt in 1868. It created a shortcut between Europe and Asia and allowed people and goods to travel more quickly and easily.

Chapter 4

The Panama Canal

The Panama Canal is known as an industrial wonder. It cuts through the middle of Panama, and connects the Atlantic and Pacific Oceans. It is 77 kilometres long, and thousands of ships use it every year.

Before the Panama Canal was built, ships travelled around Cape Horn at the bottom of South America to get from one side of North America to the other.

When the Panama Canal was finished, it became quicker and easier to transport materials and goods.

The Panama Canal was built over one hundred years ago. At that time it was the most incredible building project ever attempted. In fact, many experts did not believe it could be done. So, how was this modern wonder actually built?

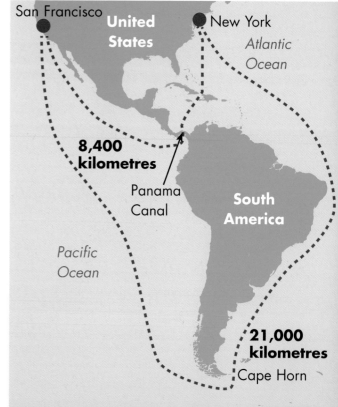

A grand idea

In 1513, the Spanish explorer Balboa trekked across Panama from north to south. At the end of his journey, he saw the Pacific Ocean. This discovery made people wonder if a canal could be built to connect the Atlantic and Pacific.

The first attempt

In 1882, the French decided to build the much-talked-about canal. Unfortunately, there were many difficulties to overcome. These included hazardous **terrain**, dangerous waterways, including the Chargus River that often flooded, poor living conditions and a harsh tropical climate that brought with it malaria and yellow fever.

Finally, in 1888 the French admitted they had failed. They had spent almost $300 million, and about 20,000 workers had died.

Find out more

The French **engineer** in charge of building the Panama Canal had already built the Suez Canal. How are these two canals similar? How are they different?

The United States takes over

In 1904, the United States took over. American engineer John Wallace led the project. But his team soon faced great challenges.

The large amount of soil being dug up had to be removed from the construction site. This made progress very slow. Workers still battled disease and harsh conditions. By June 1905, three-quarters of the workers had left the site. Wallace resigned, and again it looked like the project would fail.

The project continues

In July 1905, John Stevens was appointed as the new chief engineer. He begain by developing an efficient, working railway. Trains were needed to bring materials to the workers and to remove the soil that was being dug up.

Next, Stevens designed a movable railway track that could be moved to where the workers needed it. He also designed a machine that could empty a load of dirt off a railway car in just ten minutes. Both of these inventions saved time and money.

A new plan

Stevens had to think of ways to stop the canal from being flooded by the Chargus River. He realised that building a flat canal at sea level would not work, since it would be threatened by floodwater.

His plan was to build a system of giant "steps", called locks, that would move boats from one level of water to another. These locks would lead up to a lake that would be created by **damming** the Chargus River. More locks would be built at the other end of the canal to take boats down again.

The idea of using locks was not new. But the locks in the Panama Canal would have to be three times bigger than any built before. Could it be done? It took four years to build all the locks. Even now, these locks are celebrated as an engineering feat.

A continuing problem

Stevens solved many problems facing the Panama Canal project, but one that persisted was the disease brought by mosquitoes.

War was declared on the insects! Workers sprayed mosquitoes with insecticide and poured oil onto **stagnant** water where they bred; workers' homes were **fumigated**, and mesh windows and doors were fitted. Eventually the disease was controlled.

Another new boss

In 1907, John Stevens resigned. George Goethals took over as chief engineer and immediately faced a new problem when his workers went on **strike**.

Digging the canal was dangerous work. Explosives were used to blast dirt and rocks. Some workers wanted higher pay for this dangerous work, but Goethals would not agree. There was a strike and digging stopped.

Goethals refused to give in and hired new replacement workers. Work on the canal resumed and continued in shifts, all day and all night.

It's open!

On 10 October 1913, an explosion removed the last barrier. Water flowed into the canal, joining the Atlantic and Pacific Oceans. On 15 August 1914, the Panama Canal officially opened with the passage of the *SS Ancon*.

Despite the problems it faced, the Panama Canal is recognised today as a wonder of the modern world.

Did you know?

Building the Panama Canal took the USA ten years and cost $350 million.

The Panama Canal today

- It takes 10 hours to travel through the canal.
- Over 13,000 ships use it each year.
- In 2010, the millionth ship passed through.
- In 2016, a new and bigger level was added to take longer container ships.

Chapter 5

Successes and failures

Most dams, bridges and canals bring great benefits to communities, cities and even whole countries. They are seen by many as a sign of progress, and something to be proud of.

But is this always the case? Unfortunately not.

Building of dams, bridges and canals can sometimes have a negative effect on people, animals and plants that live nearby. And sometimes things go terribly wrong and these **structures** fail. This can have devastating effects, especially if lives are lost.

Teton Dam disaster
5 June 1976

In November 1975, the building of the Teton Dam in Idaho was finally complete. The much-needed dam was built to store water for **irrigation**, and to stop flooding along the Teton River. But excitement about the building of the dam did not last long. … Just over six months later, the unthinkable happened. The dam collapsed.

In the early hours of the morning, a small leak grew into a gush of water that burst through the dam wall. The water exploded out of the enormous dam with extraordinary speed and power. The result was a massive disaster.

The fast-flowing water destroyed everything in its path. Towns were flattened, 11 people were killed, thousands of people were left homeless and $400 million worth of damage was reported.

The failure of the Teton Dam is one of the worst engineering disasters in US history. So, why did it happen? Investigations found that a combination of reasons, including the type of soil used, failing to waterproof rocks used in the dam, and not repairing small leaks, caused the collapse.

Did you know?

In 1889, a dam in Philadelphia, US, burst and 10,000 people were killed.

A bridge in the news

The Westgate Bridge is the second longest bridge in Australia. It is located in Melbourne and spans the Yarra River, joining the city area with the western suburbs. It featured in the news for tragic reasons.

16 October 1970

SHOCKING BRIDGE COLLAPSE

Yesterday the half-built West Gate Bridge collapsed and plunged into the Yarra River.

Thirty-two workers are dead, four men are missing and many more have been injured. Rescue workers worked late into the night searching for the missing men.

At 11.50 in the morning workers heard the frightening sound of bolts popping and snapping followed by a series of massive explosions, as concrete cracked and steel twisted. A large section of the unfinished bridge broke away and crashed into the water below.

George Bastecky saw the bridge collapse as he sat in his office. He recalled the horrific event. "The bridge section was left dangling at a crazy angle. It was like slow motion. Then it collapsed in a heap of rubble. The bang was monstrous. It shook me out of my chair. I saw flames burst into the air."

All Australians are shocked at the horror of this tragic accident. The government has promised to hold an inquiry to find out why it happened.

No one knows if and when work will continue on the bridge.

Eight years later, the Westgate Bridge was in the news again – this time for all the right reasons. It was finally opened! Two years after the horrific tragedy, work restarted on the bridge, and by 1978 it was complete. This time, there were no mistakes. Construction of the bridge took into account the lessons learned from the collapse. New safety rules for workers were also put in place after the disaster. Today, the bridge provides an important link between the east and west sections of Melbourne.

Dams

Positive outcomes
- Prevents flooding of the river
- Stores water for use during times of **drought**
- Provides places for recreation such as water-skiing
- Water can be used to create **hydroelectricity**
- Stored water can be used to irrigate farmland and provide drinking water to towns and cities

Bridges

Positive outcomes
- People can easily and quickly travel over canyons, rivers and streams
- Travel time is reduced
- Bridge-building projects create many new jobs
- Communities that were isolated become connected to larger towns or cities
- Traffic can be diverted away from villages, towns and communities, which reduces traffic, making it easier for people to travel locally

Negative outcomes
- Homes need to be knocked down to make way for the dam
- If a dam breaks, flooding can occur
- Dams affect the migration patterns of wildlife such as fish and birds
- When the natural flow of water is changed, plants can die and other creatures are affected

Negative outcomes
- Increased traffic across bridges leads to more pollution in these areas
- In some cases, homes need to be moved to make way for the new bridge and communities are destroyed
- When a new bridge is built, natural **habitats** are destroyed or changed and animals lose their homes
- Bridge building is dangerous work and can result in injury or death

Canals

Positive outcomes

- Ships and boats can travel to more places, easily and safely
- Travel time is reduced
- An increased amount of goods can be transported
- Jobs are created in the construction and operation of the canal
- Tourism increases, bringing money to towns and cities along the canal

Negative outcomes

- Increased shipping activity means more pollution
- Some people's homes are destroyed to make room for the canal
- Natural habitats are lost when land is cleared for canals
- Canal building can be dangerous and result in loss of life
- Increased tourism can lead to more rubbish and waste

Conclusion

Dams, bridges and canals began as simple **structures** that were designed to help people solve problems – to store water, to get from one place to another or to irrigate crops.

Today, dams, bridges and canals are complex structures. Dams are large enough to store water or make electricity for the use of whole cities. Bridges can **span** great distances and carry heavy traffic. Canals are large enough to join oceans and carry massive ships.

Building these structures is an enormous task that involves many people over many years. They have improved the way people live, and some have become famous landmarks.

Glossary

channel	a long gutter or groove
damming	to hold back with a barrier
drought	a long period of dry weather
engineer	a designer or builder
fumigated	when smoke or gas is used to destroy pests
habitat	a place where a plant or animal naturally grows or lives
hydroelectricity	electricity that is produced by water power
irrigation	artificial watering of land to grow plants
redirect	to change the direction of something
span	to extend across
stagnant	not flowing
strike	to stop work until the people in charge agree to demands
structure	something that is built
suspension	when something is hung
terrain	the physical features of land

Index